January 2004

tHE
ABC OF ViCE

An Insatiable Women's Guide, Alphabetized

For Wendy! Here's to laughing out loud! Love! Gene

BY NICOLE HOLLANDER & REGINA BARRECA

The ABC of Vice
The Insatiable Women's Guide

Text by Regina Barreca   Illustrations by Nicole Hollander

Copyright 2003 Regina Barreca and Nicole Hollander
Published by Bibliopola Press, UConn Co-op, Storrs, CT, 06269-2019
Distributed by the University Press of New England,
Hanover, N.H. 03755-2048
Manufactured in the United States

Library of Congress Cataloging-in-Publication Data is available.

ISBN   0-939883-11-2

Book and cover design: Jennifer Weinland

is FOR

AduLtery

THis is A biG Vice becAuse Nobody iN HeR RiGHt MiNd WANts to be tHe otHeR WOMAN but some of the nicest women you know are or once were. Adultery is scary because it leads to lying, which is another vice, including women lying to their girlfriends, something nearly impossible under most situations, saying even to best friends **"No, we just work together. I'm not even attracted to him"** when in fact they dream hourly about starting a new life with the guy and having him build a house with his own hands in the country where she will stencil the walls, something also impossible to justify. Adultery is a bigger deal for women than for men for two reasons: 1. since we don't (any longer) like having unsafe sex with strangers, we therefore form relationships with the man in question which makes for a mess if he or we are married (not to each other although that can happen, too, trust us); 2. he rarely leaves his wife and even when he does leave his wife he usually marries a nineteen year old named Bambi (or Bunny or Gazelle, some woodland creature) or Misty (or Raine or Sunny, some weather pattern). **When involved in adultery, women will often get parts of their bodies waxed more often than they vacuum the rug;** it also involves changing the sheets a lot. We think it is not worth the bother, even when the man is very attractive.

A is FOR ADULTERY
A is FOR ADULTERY
No, MY DARLING, I CAN'T GET TO THE MOTEL RIGHT THIS MINUTE ... I'VE GOT TO PICK UP MY KIDS AT SOCCER. WHAT ABOUT MONDAY? YOU'VE GOT A MEETING, ALL DAY? HOW DOES NOVEMBER LOOK?
A is FOR ADULTERY
A is FOR ADULTERY
A is FOR ADULTERY
A is FOR ADULTERY
A is FOR ADULTERY
A is FOR ADULTERY

is FOR

BRAS

You keep telling yourself that you will get a bra that fits exactly the way it is supposed to but this will never happen. Especially now when you actually need undergarments, which you didn't until you were thirty-eight, but underwear for women is only designed to fit the female body up to but not including age thirty-eight. Unless you have resigned yourself to buy big white brassieres from a catalog, the ones that hoist your breasts up and practically swing them over your shoulders, you will be disappointed. **Cute bras will look cute as long as they do not actually touch your person.** Even when you gather up enough courage to be measured by the official Lingerie Lady **(a.k.a.: "Ilsa of the S.S.")** you end up leaving with a garment as useless as it is painful. You once bought a cheap brassiere ($7.95 on sale) in 1987 and it fit perfectly but they stopped making that model. All contemporary bras fit their wearers for the first fifteen minutes after which they partake of the **"shrink-wrap"** effect whereby body temperature causes the elastic under your breasts and in the shoulder straps to wither and tighten. The tops of your tits begin to grow like muffins out of a tin and you begin to itch uncontrollably in the middle of your back.

Front-closure bras, apparently a good idea, have the unfortunate tendency to pop unexpectedly, **causing your breasts to fling themselves into the dinner plate.** Sometimes it will not even be your own dinner plate. Sports bras are good but funny under formal wear, especially strapless satin gowns.

is FOR

CHOCOLATE

the insatiable women's diary · ALPHABETIZED.

In a world where most people think "ARUGALA" is what the background singers are chanting in "The Lion Sleeps Tonight," it's interesting that chocolate remains a singularly knowable and nameable food passion. Children who haven't yet memorized their home address or last name know how to differentiate between an Almond Joy and a Mounds bar. The average American loves her chocolate, despite the fact that one chocolate sprinkle has as many calories as, say, a side of beef. To say that people "love" their chocolate is not hyperbolic. The word "love" is used here in the same way it's used in wedding vows and other

PAGE 15

sacred rituals, such as opera: we're talking about devotion, loyalty, the acknowledgment of eccentric tastes, and an overwhelming sense of connection to others in the same state of mind. This is because chocolate is as much fun as most other vices, sometimes more.

Why associate chocolate with vice? Because there's something selfish, extravagant, and messy about both sin and chocolate. **Neither is good for you, but that doesn't stop your appetites.** Neither is something you ever need – but both you can want so much you think about them until you can almost taste them on your tongue, your mouth watering slightly at the very idea. They involve texture, taste, melting, not wanting to share, and the necessity to clean up afterwards. Often the aftermath involves guilt, heightened sensitivity, and shame, as well as a deep sense of secret, very personal pleasure. Many people also feel a need to hide the evidence but give themselves away by smiling a lot.

C is FOR CHOCOLAte C is FOR CHOCOLAte
CHERRY
CHOCOLATE
CREME FILING WITH FLOATING PIECES OF SILVERED ALMOND.
JUST A SUGGESTION... HERSHEY'S KISSES WITH CHERRIES AND SLIVERED ALMONDS? NO, I DON'T THINK IT WOULD BE TOO CROWDED.
C is FOR CHOCOLATE C is FOR CHOCOLATE
C is FOR CHOCOLATE C is FOR CHOCOLATE
C is FOR CHOCOLATE C is FOR CHOCOLATE

is FOR

Dieting

to spend Good worry time over whether or not you are retaining water is useful only if you are a boat. We used to agree, secretly, with Helen Rowland, the turn-of-the-century writer who quipped that "from the day on which she weighs 140, the chief excitement of a woman's life consists in spotting women who are fatter than she is." We'd look at other women and try to guess their weight as if we were **at a State Fair trying to win a prize.** We have come to the conclusion, however, that we really are loved, or respected, or admired, for ourselves alone and not our finely-honed thighs, or firm buttocks, or steel bust, or toned upper arms.

If somebody likes our style, they like our style. They'll take you fifteen pounds over, ten pounds under, whatever, because it's incidental, not essential. Here, have a cookie.

is FOR

ENVY

PeNis-eNVY we don't HAVE, ALtHOUGH we wouLdN't Mind some of tHe beNefits AWARded to tHose MeMbeRs: full access to the power structure, political influence, a decent credit line, and the ability to walk into a garage without the mechanic grinning and thinking "Oh, good, now I can put that wing on my house" because we have a question about the transmission. (The best story I ever heard as an antidote to Freud concerns a little girl who, when seeing her naked infant brother for the first time, merely commented "Isn't it a good thing, Mommy, that it isn't on his face?").

E IS FOR ENVY

I MUST HAVE MORE SHOES THAN IMELDA MARCOS, MORE HUSBANDS THAN THE GABORS, BIGGER BREASTS THAN NICOLE SMITH...

-AND A FAMILY EVEN MORE LOVING AND DYSFUNCTIONAL THAN THE OSBOURNES.

is FOR

FLiRtAtion

WHEN done CORRECTLY, FLIRTATION IS A WORK OF ART; FLIRTATION can be both creative and inspiring. It is the peripheral vision of the heart. During those passages of life where you feel you are playing to an empty house, a healthy dose of flirtation can assure you that you not only have an audience, but that you hold center stage. Flirtation is about arousal, not satiation. You dream of him. Long, ripe dreams of soft mouths and liquifying limbs, of fingertips against satin and then, soon, against skin. Hands in his hair and the slackness of his lips as he looks at you from across the room. Umm, umm, umm.

Unfortunately, however, not many people learn how to flirt properly. Grabbing is not part of flirtation; neither is thrusting your tongue down somebody's throat as if you were sticking your hand into a mailbox. Flirtation depends on oblique hints, slight innuendo, brief glimpses, and nearly imperceptible suggestions of impropriety. **It also depends on timing: you have to know when to stop flirting;** too often the ritual is prolonged past the point where it becomes wearisome. You want to end the flirtation before one of the parties stops sending unsigned valentines and starts filing for restraining orders.

F is FOR FLIRTATION
MADMOISELLE, it's RAINING... ALLOW ME to CARRY YOUR POODLE.
WHY SIR... I DON'T believe we KNOW EACH other WELL ENOUGH FOR ME to ALLOW YOU to CARRY MY POODLE.

is FOR

GLuttony

It's difficult to imagine how an apparently

amateur evil like gluttony got onto a list with big-time sins like envy and greed. Chowing down at the Pizza Hut salad bar doesn't mean anyone else will go hungry that night because of your hankering for croutons. **Eating forty-six canapés** (without even knowing how to pronounce the word) at a work-related social event is probably better than positioning yourself next to the bar, asking them to fill you up with single-malt scotch and then driving home. If you stuff yourself, the worse that will happen is that you will feel as if you could expand enough to fill a rumpus room by merely breathing deeply. But nobody else will be damaged.

After the break-up of an affair isn't it as **perfectly acceptable to eat an entire bag of Hershey's kisses in one sitting** as it is to rent *Brief Encounter* and *Moonstruck* during one trip to the video store? How can it hurt? (By the way, if it's the end of a long-term relationship you are then allowed to eat everything in the house that doesn't move or have a given name since your only secure belief at the moment is that no one will ever love you anyway, pretty much ruling out the idea that you will have to show your naked body to a stranger ever again. When you're facing eternal solitude **what's the harm in ingesting an unfrozen Sara Lee cheesecake?**)

And the seducers in this crowd are for the most part a little too cute to be regarded as Satan's spawn. Who's there on the sidelines tempting us into gluttony? Betty Crocker? Aunt Jemima? The Keebler Elves? Orvil Redenbacher?

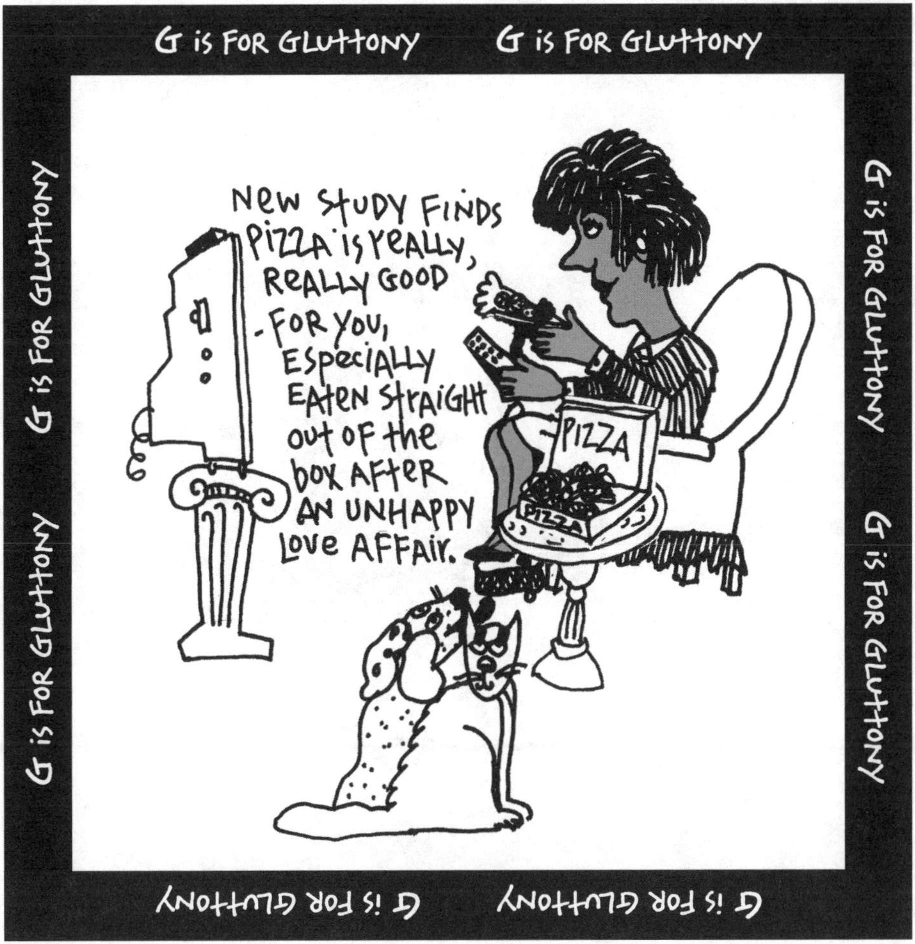

is FOR

HoteLs

We suGGest tHAt you ALWAys stAy At the best HoteL possibLe, even if that means selling your body to the night. Or worse, clipping coupons. Tawdry hotel rooms are a leading cause of depression among women over thirty, according to experts. **We are experts, believe us.** Have you ever stayed in one of those miserable places whose walls remind you of your elementary school? Where the scent of wet wool, old feet, and cheap soap mingle, shall we say, infelicitously? Where your soul shrivels at the very idea of bathing, or sleeping, or even touching the remote to turn on the television? Where, by the end of your stay, you are practically squatting in the corner, dribbling and helpless, like an extra from *"The Snake Pit"* but without Olivia DeHaviland to prove that life may once again, someday, offer the possibility of joy? Don't stay in such places. Find a hotel that supplies you with cute accessories, a plush terry robe, and chocolates on the pillow. It doesn't matter if one night's tariff is the equivalent of your take-home pay for the week. **Isn't your sanity worth it?**

Hi, Room Service?
Howya doin'?
I'm GREAT! Just
stepped outta the
tub ... wrapped
in one of those
Fluffy cashmere
robes you provide.
I'm wondering
if you could send
up 3 SHRIMP COCK-
TAILS AND A SPLIT
OF CHAMPAGNE?
In the little
Fridge? You're
kidding!

is FOR

INCONSIDERATE BASTARDS

THESE ARE OCCASIONALLY HELPFUL IN YOUR LIFE, EVEN IF THAT IS HARD TO BELIEVE. If you are a adult woman and keep an inconsiderate bastard around, consider the purpose he serves. Perhaps you are like our friend Victoria who says (and we quote): "My first husband and I screamed at each other for three years. Those turned out to be years that were very productive for me because when I get screamed at I get scared and when I get scared, I work. I got tenure then I got a divorce. If I'm nearing a deadline for an article, sometimes I'll call my ex-husband."

the **ABC** *of* Vice

I is FOR INCONSIDERATE BASTARDS

So last week this inconsiderate bastard aces me out of a parking space. I had to drive around for forty-five minutes!

Finally I park. As I get out of the car, I slip on a diamond ring... I track down the sweet old couple who lost it and as a reward, they give me a villa in Greece.

is FOR

JUNK

It is impossible to understand why people Like what they Like as it is to understand why they like WHO they like. What is junk to you might be a treasure to somebody else. (See "(e)x-husbands.")

is for

KNOWLEDGE OF HAIRSTYLISTS

WANT to KNOW the best thiNG About A Good HAiRCut? It does Not MAKE you CRY. Pam and I both happened to be living in London in our early twenties. We went to a chic salon offering inexpensive styling on days when the staff was trained. Pam and I both had waist-length blankets of wavy hair. When the stylist began to work on Pam, he began by discussing her as if she were a patient under heavy anesthetic. "Look at the dry yet oddly lanky texture of the hair. **Notice the way it makes her face look square.** Consider the fact, too, that the color of her hair is so dull it is almost unnatural." At this point, Pam could no longer contain her tears. Silently at first, but with growing passion, she started to weep.

She didn't move. Neither did I. She and I were still sniffling when we left. **Pam looked like cross between a Persian lamb and Maria Schneider and I looked like a cross between a poodle and Art Garfunkle.** Ironically, nobody else seemed to think we looked all that different.

I thought about The Heartbreaking Haircut because I went to a fancy salon in Manhattan. On my way to lunch with a couple of editors, I figured it might be fun to see if one of the stylists could take a look me. He looked at me all right: I immediately recognized the same voracious glint that I saw in the eyes of the evil man in London. This time I knew enough to leave. Fast. There are things to cry about in life. Someone's imperfect knowledge of what looks best on the top of your head is not one of them.

K is FOR KNOWLEDGE OF HAIRSTYLISTS
I've waiting ALL MY Life to cut your Hair.

is FOR

LUST

LuSt CAN

be GReAt.

Absolutely fabulous. Terrific. It can get you moving with the thumping persistence of the **Energizer bunny.** It can wake you up out of a physical slumber and suddenly remind you of the wonders of the flesh–the sheer joy of having fingertips and eyelashes and skin. **Aroused,** we can feel as if every single piece of us is being put into play (and as if we can play with every single piece). Just as every generation thinks it's elders sat around carving wheels out of stone while the earth's crust cooled, every generation thinks it invented lust, but that kind of thinking is as cute as it is false. As long as people have been creating music, telling stories, or making pictures, lust has been a primary player. Operas are about lust at least as much as they're about love; literature is shot through with lust; the greatest art elevates lust, refining it into gorgeous bodies reflecting a benevolent and joyous Maker. Lust isn't confined to the young or the attractive. We heard stories about it from the nursery onwards. The prince waking Snow White with a kiss has to do with the powers of lust, which is why the wicked stepmother was so aggravated. **The big, bad wolf waiting for Red Riding Hood could be a guy with a Harley making his motor purr outside your window.** Get onto the back of that bike. Lust can pour warmth into a life that has chilled under enforced indifference and resurrect passion.

Trust us.

is FOR

MAybe

MAybe I SHOULdN't SAY tHis, but...

1. You can be an absolutely wonderful person but that doesn't guarantee the person you love best will love you back.

2. You can be an absolutely wonderful person and make a great impression but that doesn't necessarily mean you'll get the job.

3. Glasses do not make everyone look intelligent.

4. Just because it is on sale doesn't necessarily mean it's a bargain.

5. Just because you *can* do it doesn't necessarily mean you *should* do it.

6. When you do nice things for people what will most often happen is that you will be asked to do more nice things for people.

7. Flat shoes can be as painful as high heels.

8. No one is interested in how many calories you consumed in any given time period.

9. Eating fiber does not in and of itself make you morally superior to your peers.

10. Not everybody loves a parade.

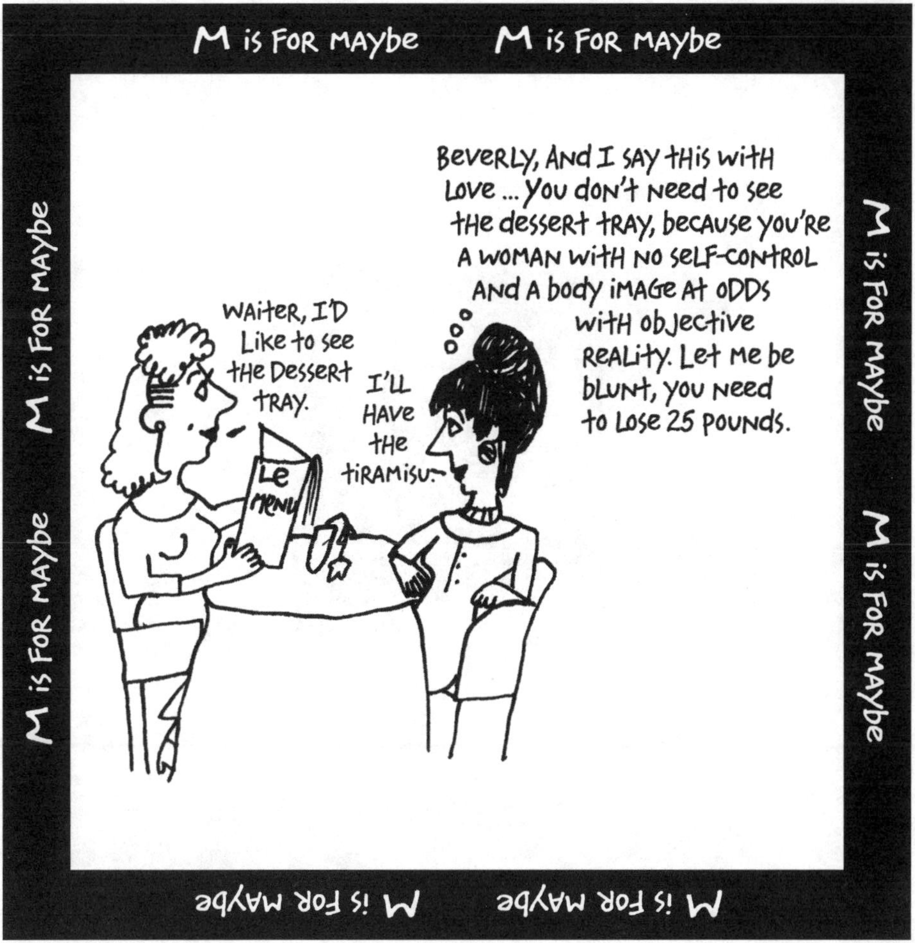

is FOR

NAPPiNG

NAPPING is NATURE'S WAY OF GETTING YOU into

tip-top SHAPE. Haven't lots of big executives and great thinkers extolled naps as the key to their enormous success? Wasn't there just a magazine article about this? Look for the magazine. **Decide it is time to go through the stacks of magazines you've accumulated over the past weeks.** Months. Pause to look at other articles that might also help you get to your goal quicker. (NOT THE IMMEDIATE GOAL OF NAPPING, BUT THE LARGER GOAL FOR WHICH NAPPING WILL PREPARE YOU.) Hunt for scissors with which to cut out some of the more useful articles. Decide it would be good to start a file where you know you could find these articles. Look through your old filing cabinet for a file you aren't actively using so that you can start this new important file. Decide it is time to organize your filing cabinet. **Eventually, fall asleep on the floor, covered by clippings.**

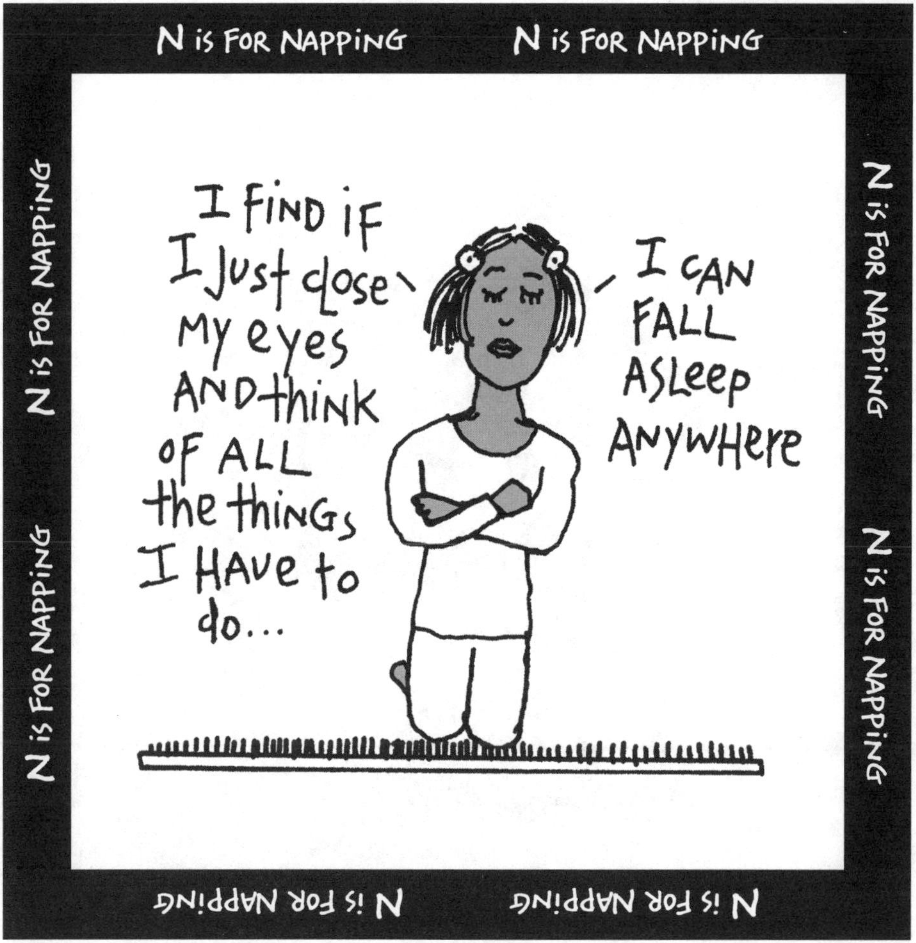

is FOR

ORGANIZING

WE HAVE FRIENDS WHOSE CLOSETS HAVE NOT been NEATLY ORGANIZED since the CARTER AdMINISTRATION. Yet we do not have the right to go and insist they alphabetize their garments. This is true even if they insist on keeping clothing so old, so unusable, and so tattered they could be donated, not to Goodwill, but to the Smithsonian. Everybody has one place they clean that nobody else in the world even notices, which also implies that everybody has at least one place they don't even think of cleaning which everybody else in the world scrubs down. **Perhaps you scrub out every bath and shower stall you step into**, which actually seems like quite a good idea when you think about it. But then you'll go and drink out of someone else's glass, finish what's left on their plate, use their cutlery, or try their lipstick. Others would not finish someone else's food even if seated at the Last Supper. Avoid annoying those you love by organizing their lives or their closets for them.

O is FOR ORGANIZING OTHER PEOPLE'S CLOSETS
No, I DON'T Need HELP ORGANIZING MY CLOSET...
EVER SINCE I DISCOVERED ALIENS WERE COLONIZING IN THERE, I STORE MY CLOTHES ON THE BED.

is FOR

Pride

PRide, we'Re HAPPY to ANNouNce, doesn't come eAsily to us. We're terrible at pride. Shame, guilt, a squirming sense of undeserving – now those we've got a real talent for; we could teach workshops in "Low self-esteem" although nobody would want to sign up for them. If pride is truly the considerable vice everybody says it is – many claim pride is the big original sin, coming before the fall, sort of like winter fashions – then we're all set for heaven. Saying we're all set for heaven, however, smacks of boasting, so we're still unsaved. Pride is the most confusing of vices. **Unlike lust or envy, pride seems as much a virtue as a vice.** If we are too proud to behave like cowards, or hypocrites, or a cheapskates, then pride has saved us from worse sins; if we are too proud to be vicious, callous, or vengeful, then **pride has offered itself to us as the least of all evils, a little bit of possible wickedness injected into our lives** the way a little bit of a virus is injected in an inoculation to ward off graver illness.

When Pride shows up like a character out of Edgar Allen Poe, however, all dressed up and ready to defy mortality itself, then it might indeed be a good time to edge your way out the door.

is for

Quintessentially

Fabulous bath experiences

Quintessentially Fabulous

bath experiences are unrivaled by other pleasures. Steamy sex is good; steamy baths last longer. And you can, after all, **refill the tub.**

is FOR

ReAL EState

Let's FACE it: AFter A certAiN AGe,

ReAL estAte becomes sexy. How is real estate like sex?

You start to think about getting it, where it will be, what you'll do with it once you have it; you imagine it's shape, texture, and impact on your life. You wonder what your friends will think. **Some individuals become obsessed with it; they want it no matter where it is**, what shape it's in, or even if it will cost them more than it's worth. Others are so committed to one and only one that they read endless articles about how to preserve it, how to jazz it up, how to update it so it doesn't go out of style, and how to tweak it here and there so it remains a source of delight. **Real estate becomes sexy because it's about physical comfort and bodily pleasure, and it seems to create an appetite for itself.** That's why it's fascinating to see what other people have and what they've done with it.

is FOR

SHoes

IF YOU WANT to CHEER YOURSELF UP,

do not go to a fancy, upscale shoe boutique and look for a mark-down on high-priced footwear. Remind yourself that they are only selling what no one *sane* bought. When I came home from a fabulous sale, having spent a whole purse full of savings on a pair of purple monstrosities, an old boyfriend said slowly, and with a little sigh, "You would wear a suit of armor more often than you'll be able to wear those." I dumped the guy and, much later, gave away the shoes. His comment remains essentially valid.

That's the trouble with buying things on sale, or under sale circumstances: you think you're getting a bargain even though - - most of the time - - you are not. Remember this enduring fact of life: when you're thinking **"Wow! I can pay just forty dollars for two hundred dollar boots!"** You should be thinking "Gee, earlier this season, some poor soul paid two hundred dollars for a pair of forty dollar boots."

S is FOR SHOES S is FOR SHOES
S is FOR SHOES S is FOR SHOES
S is FOR SHOES S is FOR SHOES
S is FOR SHOES S is FOR SHOES
I'M IN PAIN... therefore I'M LOOKING FABULOUS.

is FOR

teLePHONes

We spent our youth sitting next to telephones waiting for a call from The Planet of the Boys. We spent hours sweating next to the phone like convicts waiting for the governor's reprieve. A friend sent us a card involving a new service: Call Thwarting. **Call Thwarting guarantees: "No more two a.m. calls to his apartment, with the promise to hang up if a woman answers.** No calling just to see if anyone picks up. No continuous ringing and disturbing the neighbors." How about calling the operator to see if your own phone is working (just in case he can't get through)? Call Thwarting: An idea whose time had come.

Now that we're grown-up, this doesn't happen, right? No more waiting for the call, no more checking to see if there's a message, no more repeatedly playing the messages for girlfriends to see if they can decipher the hidden meaning beneath the phrase "I'll call later"?

Guess again. All the finger-chewing, lip-biting, mind-numbingly energy has been funneled onto *waiting for phone calls from The Planet of Professional Contacts.* Now we torture ourselves by wondering "Should I call the editor **now or wait until I know she's at lunch? Is it right to leave a friendly please-please-***please*-**get-back-to-me-so-that-I-can-get-on-with-my-life message on her voice mail?** Is this editor the one that has the sort of voice mail where you can listen to the message you've just left in order to check whether or not you sound tragically insecure? Should I try to call her early tomorrow so that she'll think I'm a bright morning person even though I am no such thing?" Call us sentimental, call us neurotic, call us crazy, but call us.

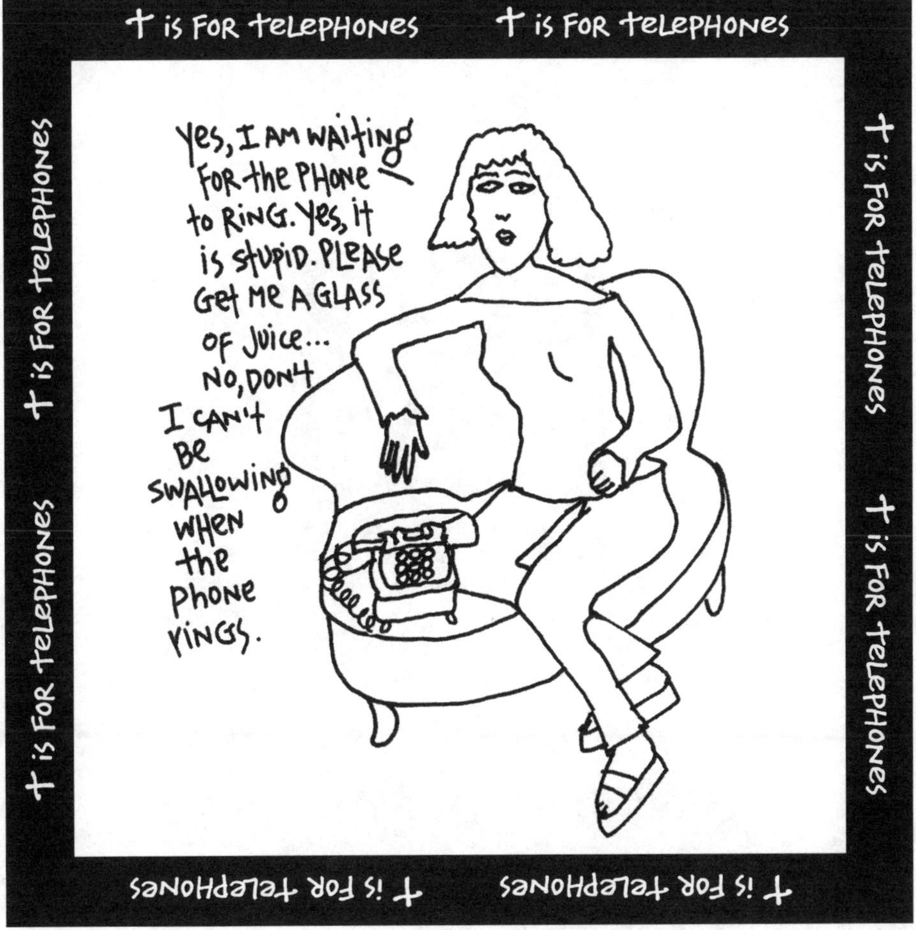

is FOR

UNCONditioNAL LoVe

We were well into the prime of life before

discovering one GREAt tRUtH:

even unconditional love has conditions.

the **ABC** *of* Vice

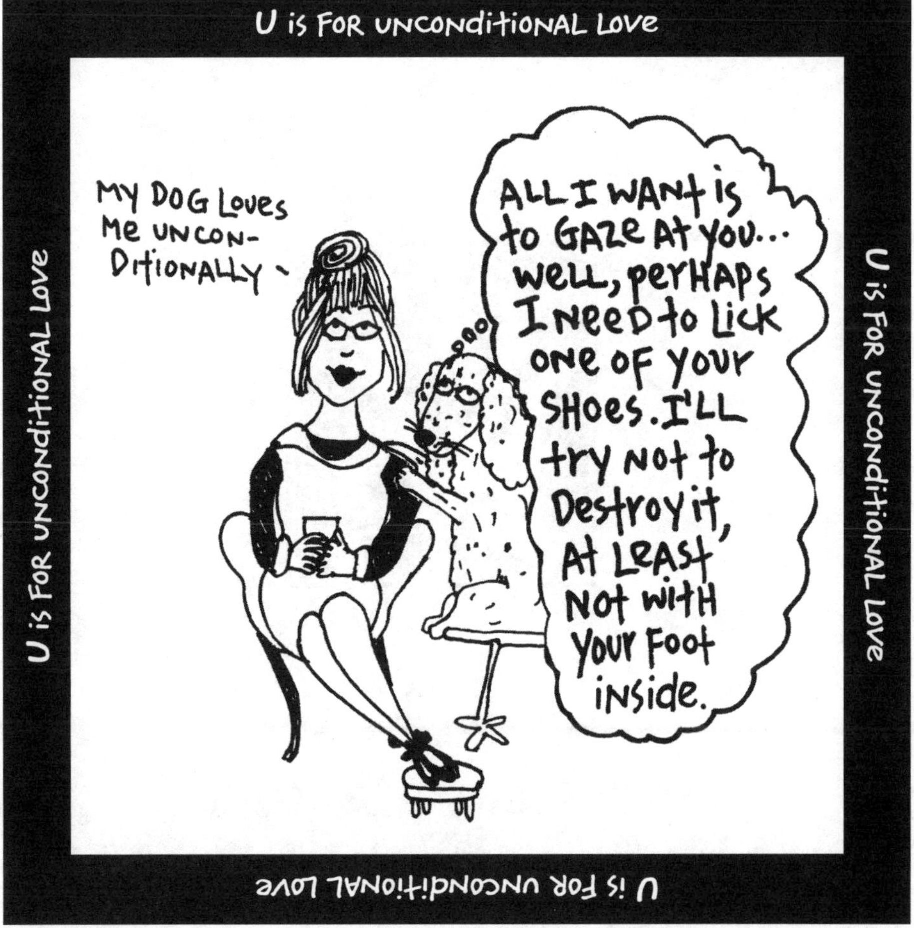

is FOR

VICARIOUS PLEASURE

JUST AS "NOUVEAU RICHE" IS bETTER THAN NO

RICHE AT ALL, so is vicarious happiness better than no happiness at all. Okay, it happened to somebody else, not to you, but being happy for somebody else is - - on certain days - - as close as you're going to get. We do not think that being happy makes you a moron. **Happiness is more than a tool for survival - - at it's best moments, it becomes an act of redemption.** It allows us to redeem moments that might otherwise have been lost to pain or despair - - being able to laugh is sometimes more about working through an issue than it is about avoiding or treating it lightly. Laughter is, after all, the most human of activities

- - it's one of the few things people do that animals do not (the other activities that animals do not perform involve applying artificial fingernails and **singing out loud to Aretha Franklin's "Respect" on the car radio).**

V is FOR VICARIOUS PLEASURE
Me? I'M stuck At the office. WHAT Are you up to?
SHreDDING ALL that tAX stuFF you're supposed to HANG on to... pouring MAPLE syrup on your rollodex AND your P.D.A. Great! CALL me LATER.

is for

(ex) wife

IF you ARE AN ex-wiFe,

ReAd tHis:

the floozies he sees now are women who flounce through life with ankle bracelets, feather boas and alligator shoes. They are taking him for a ride. They cannot hold a candle to you. There are long dreams of you.

If your partner had an ex-wife read this: So WHAT if there are dreams of her? **Everybody has nightmares. And you're the one smiling on the pillow the next morning.**

If you have not ever been or ever had in your life an ex-wife read this:
YOU WIN!! **SMART COOKIE!** TAKE THE BLUE RIBBON AND RUN TO THE FRONT OF THE LINE!

is FOR

(e)x-HusbAND (s)

Is your "ex" described by one of the following?:

1. "He wanted me to have my own life, so that we would strengthen our relationship by not only looking into each other's eyes, but at the world around us. I told him that life was not a museum or an auction, where you have to be looking all around in case somebody else catches sight of something you've missed. He was very afraid of missing something. Especially if somebody else might NOT have missed it."

2. **"I wanted him to feel good about himself, know that he was attractive.** And then he came to believe that

women, all women, would love him, because I loved him, and so came to resent my claim on him. As if somehow I were in the way. He fell as in love with my idea of him. He came to believe he was too good for me."

3. "I found him annoying."

Aren't you glad he is no longer bothering you? Even if another woman is happy (or seems to be happy) to have him, **just remember that YOU no longer have to deal with his stuff.** Recall this fact often and employ it as an occasion to celebrate.

If you have more than one ex-husband, stop now. However many you have had up until this point, you have had enough.

iS FOR

YOUTH

ONce, A LONG, LONG time AGo, we thoUGHt A PeRsON stopped doiNG some thiNGs ANd stARted doiNG otHeRs AFteR A ceRtAiN AGe.

We believed that, one day, a person would stop crying in public, stop worrying about her weight, and stop getting crushes on nearly-perfect strangers. We figured that once you started menopause, you stopped breaking out.

Turns out that none of this is true.

You still stare in the mirror at night before you go to sleep and hope you'll look better in the morning. You still raise your eyebrows and smile at your reflection in a manner wholly unlike any expression you have ever created in a natural setting. You still lie awake at night wondering if somebody you really like likes you back. You still wake up hoping against hope that there will be a snow day, a fire-drill, or some kind of diversion from the usual routine. **And you still hope that your snotty, stuck-up, prettier friend will come down with a virulent case of dandruff, b.o., and bad breath,** as well as an intense itch affecting an unseemly part of her person.

Sure, you go through a lot of changes in your life between sixteen and sixty. But very little is any different. Here are the differences: as you get older, you laugh more, you learn that what you thought was self-indulgence is actually a technique for survival, and you are NEVER tempted to buy orange lipstick no matter what the magazine writers say.

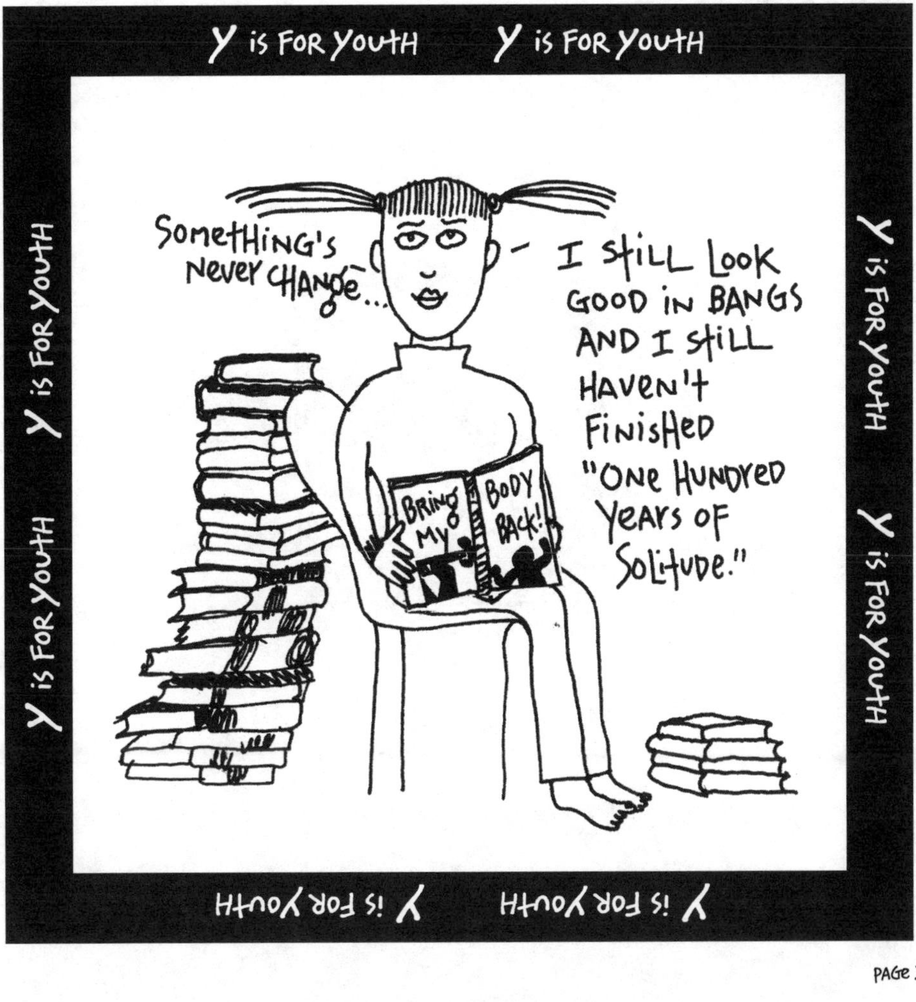

iS FOR

Zip-LoCK BAGS

Zip-Lock Bags Are the perfect product.

You can put your make-up in them and not worry about smearing eyeliner on the inside of your purse. They allow you to see what you have and where it is, too, instead of clawing around in a small floral bag like an addict looking for a hit. You can put wet bathing suits into them instead of steaming up your trunk and everything in it, like your new straw hat, on the way back from the beach. **You can pack clothes into the larger ones and smoosh out the air** when you travel in order to save room and make it less unpleasant for strange men at airports to paw through your personal ideas in the name of homeland security. You can bring several in a large purse and bring home delicious things from the buffet table at a large function. (Muffins, cookies, and cheese straws are especially good.) **You might consider having drawn into your will that your ashes should be placed in one and given to your least favorite, guilt-ridden relative or friend to carry around in his or her glove-compartment.** Few things in life would not be helped by the proper use of a zip-lock bag.

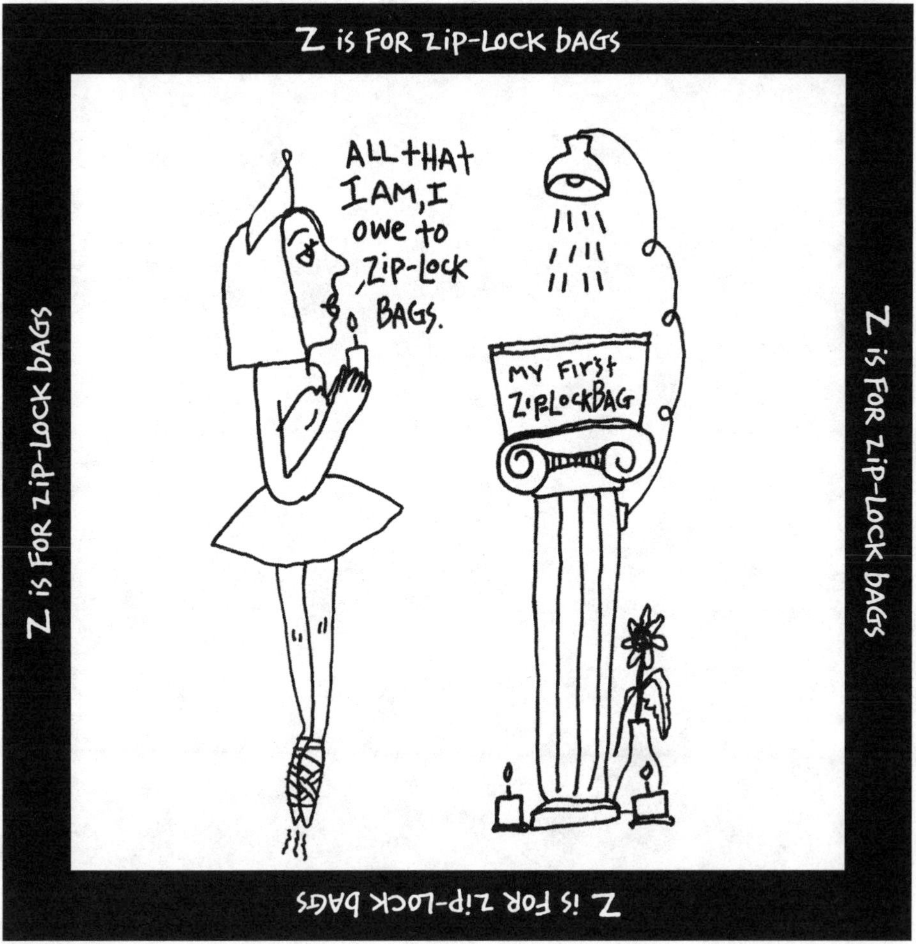

B A D   G I R L   C O U P O N

Cut Here

today buy a movie magazine and cut out pictures
of hunky guys, pin them up on the wall
all over your bed.

NO YOU ARE NOT TOO OLD FOR THIS.

Finish any ice cream in the freezer.

B A D   G I R L   C O U P O N

Cut Here

today sign up for riding lessons.
Decide to buy horse.

GET REAL!
Buy a 19th-century English print of horse in antique frame.

You come out ahead.

Will expire if you are mean to me.

Will expire if you lose more than 5 pounds.

B A D   G I R L   C O U P O N

Cut Here

today look at your house. Is it a mess?
LEAVE.
Go to a hotel for the weekend.

If its really, really out of control,
call a real estate agent and

Put it on the market.

B A D   G I R L   C O U P O N

Cut Here

today
decide to run off with
your best friend's husband ...

THEN REMEMBER HIS BAD BACK.

Forget about it.

Will expire if you lose more than 5 pounds.

Will expire if you are mean to me.

B A D   G I R L   C O U P O N

today take a bubble bath,
throw in a whole bottle of scented foaming bath oil.
soak. Read Danielle Stelle or Nora Roberts.

Later throw the book away ...

in your neighbor's garbage container.

B A D   G I R L   C O U P O N

today tell your family you're doing internet
research on 19th-century whaling practices.

CLOSE THE DOOR.

Play Sims, Doom, and Flight Simulator.

until you're in a coma.

Cut Here

Cut Here

Will expire if you are mean to me.

Will expire if you lose more than 5 pounds.

B A D   G I R L   C O U P O N

Did you buy someone
the perfect present?
Probably too good for them.

keep it for yourself,
buy them

something less expensive.

B A D   G I R L   C O U P O N

I will go with you to the plastic surgeon
when you have your eyes done and
take you home afterwards

and make you fruit smoothies
if you will tell me

I'M LUCKY I LOOK SO YOUNG.

Cut Here

Cut Here

Will expire if you lose more than 5 pounds.

Will expire if you are mean to me.

B A D G I R L C O U P O N

FOR YOUR birthday
I will GET ALL OUR FRIENDS to chip in
to send you ON AN expensive island cruise.

I may tell them you have an incurable disease
and this will be the last trip you take ...

SO TRY to LOOK WAN.

B A D G I R L C O U P O N

this COUPON entitles you to

ONE HOUR-LONG FOOt MASSAGE,

BUT NOT

FROM ME.

CUt HERE

CUt HERE

Will expire if you are mean to me.

Will expire if you lose more than 5 pounds.

B A D   G I R L   C O U P O N

today look terrific.
Buy yourself a Grande something or other.
Flirt with everyone at the coffee shop.

Give your number to an adorable 22-year-old,
so what if he/she is not

your preferred gender?

B A D   G I R L   C O U P O N

today buy a pretty recirculating fountain
for your bedroom. Fall asleep to the sound
of splashing water ... wake up at 3:00.

The sound of splashing water impels you to the bathroom.
While there decide to scrub sink, bathtub and floor.

Return Fountain.

Will expire if you lose more than 5 pounds.

Will expire if you are mean to me.

B A D   G I R L   C O U P O N

Cut Here

today ACCUSE A FRIEND OR A FAMILY MEMBER OF BORROWING A FAVORITE BLOUSE AN THEN FIND it CRUSHED AND DUSTY AT THE BACK OF YOUR CLOSET.

KEEP NAGGING THE FRIEND ABOUT

the blouse.

B A D   G I R L   C O U P O N

Cut Here

today
you MAY CRY
iN A RESTAURANT,

BUT NOT IF YOU'RE

EAtiNG WitH Me.

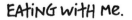

Will expire if you are mean to me.

Will expire if you lose more than 5 pounds.

B A D   G I R L   C O U P O N

tHis coupon entitles you
to wHine about your ex-Husband
or your Job

**TEN TIMES ...
Don't use them up**

ALL At once.

B A D   G I R L   C O U P O N

today I will Go sHopping witH you. You MAY LooK
in tHe MiRRoR ANd LAMent tHAt you ARe fAt, fAt,
fAt ANd I will sAY you neveR LooKed betteR,

but only if you tell me
you've always thought I had the best legs of

ALL of ouR fRiends.

Will expire if you lose more than 5 pounds.

Will expire if you are mean to me.

B A D   G I R L   C O U P O N

today buy a box
of
expensive chocolates.

Take a bite out of each one
and throw the rest away ... you may

CALL this dieting.

B A D   G I R L   C O U P O N

today CALL in sick. Go shopping. Buy a pair of
shoes that have impossibly high heels, are a size
too small and way more than you can afford,
but make your legs look fabulous.

HAVE LUNCH.

Return the shoes.

Will expire if you are mean to me.

Will expire if you lose more than 5 pounds.

Cut Here

B A D   G I R L   C O U P O N

today you may tell me the same boring story you told me last week and I will listen attentively.

I will not suggest that you are losing touch with reality or that I have something better to do than sit on the phone listening to

BORING STORIES.

Cut Here

B A D   G I R L   C O U P O N

I will go with you to the anti-cruelty society to look at puppies. I will talk you out of getting an adorable puppy, by reminding you that they do not walk themselves, and you will never again be able to have a spontaneous night out.

We will buy tropical fish instead.
You will thank me for

SAVING YOU FROM YOURSELF ... AGAIN.

Will expire if you lose more than 5 pounds.

Will expire if you are mean to me.

B A D   G I R L   C O U P O N

Cut Here

AFter your tropical FiSH die, I will HeLP you to reSeArcH backyard PooLS, WAter PLAntS AnD Koi. You will teLL Me tHAt Koi Live Forever, uNLike tropicAL FiSH.

I will remind you about raccoons and other natural predators of Koi. we will

buy SoMe PLAStic FLoWerS inSteAD.

B A D   G I R L   C O U P O N

Cut Here

todAy I WiLL Get
tAttooed.

On the way to the tattoo parlor I will talk you into getting

A PUPPY inSteAD.

Will expire if you are mean to me.

Will expire if you lose more than 5 pounds.

B A D   G I R L   C O U P O N

today you want to get
SOMETHING PIERCED.

I cannot distract you.
Okay, I will get a

NOSE RING IN SOLIDARITY.

B A D   G I R L   C O U P O N

this MONTH you will
Refuse one dinner invitation
without EXPLANATION.

DO YOU HEAR ME ?!?

No EXPLANATION.

CUT HERE

CUT HERE

the **ABC** *of* Vice

Will expire if you lose more than 5 pounds.

Will expire if you are mean to me.

B A D   G I R L   C O U P O N

YOUR SON/DAUGHTER HAS CONFIDED IN ME AND

SWORN ME TO SECRECY.

Of course I will tell you.
If they find out I told you,

YOU'RE A DEAD WOMAN.

B A D   G I R L   C O U P O N

THIS IS ONE JUST FOR YOU

_____

_____

_____

Will expire if you are mean to me.

Will expire if you lose more than 5 pounds.